Painting on silk

Pierre BRUANDET

EP PUBLISHING LIMITED

Originally published in France under the title
Peinture sur soie
Copyright © 1978 Dessain et Tolra

Translated by A. F. Hartley and Pierrick Picot

English edition copyright © 1982 EP Publishing Limited

Published by EP Publishing Limited, Bradford Road, East Ardsley, Wakefield, West Yorkshire, WF3 2JN, England
Phototypeset in England by
CTL Computer Typesetters Ltd. Leeds.

Printed and bound in Italy

ISBN 0 7158 0786 2

Where to obtain your materials

Silk
Some silks are available from good department stores as well as from craft shops. You can also contact the following suppliers:

Wm. H Bennett & Sons Ltd	MacCulloch & Wallis Ltd	Pongees Ltd	Whaleys (Bradford) Ltd
79 Piccadilly	25–26 Dering Street	184/6 Old Street	Harris Court Mills
MANCHESTER	LONDON	LONDON	Great Horton
M1 2BX	W1R 0BH	EC1V 9BP	BRADFORD
			West Yorkshire
			BD7 4EQ

Colouring materials and gutta
Many of the dyes and paints, and the gutta percha, described in this book are produced by Sennelier, a Paris firm. They may be obtained by mail order from the following importers, who will supply details and prices on request:

Atlantis Paper Co	L Cornellissen & Son
F3 Warehouse	22 Great Queen Street
New Crane Wharf	LONDON
Garnet Street	WC2B 5BH
LONDON	
E1 9QT	

Wax
This is readily available from craft shops and candlemakers' suppliers—see page 26.

Alcohol
The alcohol used (mixed with water) should be pure ethyl alcohol. Industrial alcohol, containing 5% water, is suitable but not obtainable in the UK without a permit. Medicinal alcohol may be bought without a prescription from chemists with a spirit license; it is pure alcohol. In case of difficulty surgical spirit (denatured alcohol) may be used, but methylated spirit is unsuitable, as are other solvents such as white spirit, which should *not* be used.

Contents

An introduction to painting on silk

You may have come across batik and tie-dyeing. The techniques used for these can also be used with silk. The basic principle consists of soaking the fabric in a dye bath, having first protected certain areas from the dye in some way. The pattern is created by the contrasts between the dyed and undyed areas.

Our purpose here is very different – it is to create a pattern by applying various dyestuffs onto the fabric. We focus exclusively on silk, although other fabrics, particularly wool, are also suitable.

The artists' materials and application techniques used differ according to the desired effect:

 (i) flowing designs and special effects by painting on colours which run or using cooking salt or methylated spirits.

 (ii) precise designs by using wax or gutta resists. Gutta is employed in the 'serti' technique of tracing around areas of the silk to prevent liquid dyestuffs from running.

(iii) real 'paintbrush embroideries' are produced with gouache and felt pens.

You don't need to be an expert to try your hand at painting on silk. It calls for good taste and a great deal of care, but luckily a mistake or clumsiness can often enhance the finished effect. There is nearly always a way of turning a disaster into a novel creation.

Certain techniques, such as painting the dye straight on and wax resists, can be used with very good results by children. The front cover of this book, for example, shows the work of a girl of five and a half!

Various silks and artists' materials are available in good craft shops. In case of difficulty, some sources of supply are listed on page 2.

1

2

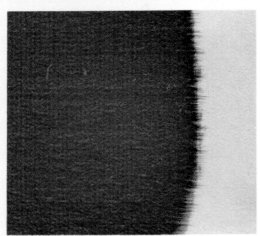

3

Silk

The word silk is applied to fabrics with a wide variety of textures. Some – chiffons, organza, crêpes—are light and rough to the touch; others, such as pongée, are smooth and shiny. Pongée, often called habutai, is sold as lining silk in many department stores.

Silk gauze and shantung are rougher and more tightly woven.

Lastly, wild silk, Indian silk, doupion and silk noile all exhibit irregularities which give them an extraordinarily rich finish.

These different qualities are obtained by varying several factors, although there is a common denominator: the origin of the raw material—the Far East. The silk thread may be fine or thick depending on the number of cocoons from which it has been spun. It may be uniform or irregular according to how it has been spun.

At the weaving stage the way in which the warp is set up on the loom and the weave plan will produce completely different finishes from one and the same thread.

If they are to be decorated, all these silks need to be free of sizing and to be specially treated so that the thread will absorb the colours fully.

It is best to choose a natural-coloured silk, i.e. white or slightly off-white.

The most commonly used silks are pongée, twill and wild silk.

You also have a choice of several weights, that is, thicknesses of fabric. Initially you are best advised to choose lightweight fabrics, for example, a fine habutai, which will allow you to study all the techniques with only a modest outlay.

The illustrations in this section show the main types of silk. These have been dyed so that their differing textures and the direction in which the dyes run can be seen more clearly.

All the photographs show the silk magnified as it appears through a pick counter.

1. *Chiffon (Mousseline)*
2. *Organza*
3. *Crêpe-de-Chine*
4. *Taffeta*
5. *Twill*
6. *Tussore*
7. *Pongée (Habutai)*
8. *Jersey*
9. *Bengadoup*
10. *Moussedoup*
11. *Silk gauze*
12. *Shantung*
13. *Wild silk*
14. *Indian silk*
15. *Doupion*
16. *Silk noile*

4

5

6

7

8

9

10

11

12

13

14

15

16

Colours for painting on silk

There are two main classes of material which can be used for painting on silk: those which run in the silk and those which do not.

1. Colours which run

These are transparent colours which flow like water, penetrating to the core of the silk fibres and acting as dyes.

A drop falling onto the tightly-stretched silk forms a patch which spreads in all directions. With some fabrics, such as wild silk, the colour runs more in one direction than in the other, thus forming bands.

Note that some shades run more than others.

Commercially available materials are normally intended for different types of user:

Professional craftspeople and decorators
These products are very highly pigmented and have to be diluted with water and alcohol (see page 2) mixed in equal quantities. The mixture–colour ratio can go up to 6-to-1 depending on how deep or how pale a colour is required.

Amateurs
Ready-to-use products. You should not exceed a ratio of 2 parts water–alcohol mixture to 1 part colour, otherwise you are liable to end up with washed-out, lifeless tones.

Children
These products are diluted with water only. Their rather slight propensity to run can be increased by means of a special product called a diffusing agent supplied by the manufacturer.

The firms which make and distribute these products have designed informative instruction cards which will enable you to make the most of the potential offered by their dyes.

The majority of the techniques for decorating silk explained in this book can be used with these products.

All these colouring materials keep well if stored in tightly-sealed glass containers. Any sediment should be removed by filtering the solution through a filter paper (e.g. a coffee filter). Sedimentation may occur with highly concentrated products and is liable to result in dark spots when the paint is applied to the silk.

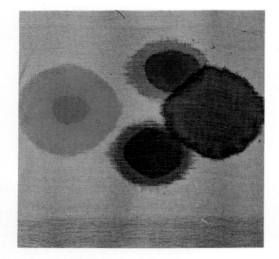

Running colours on pongée

Running colours on wild silk

8

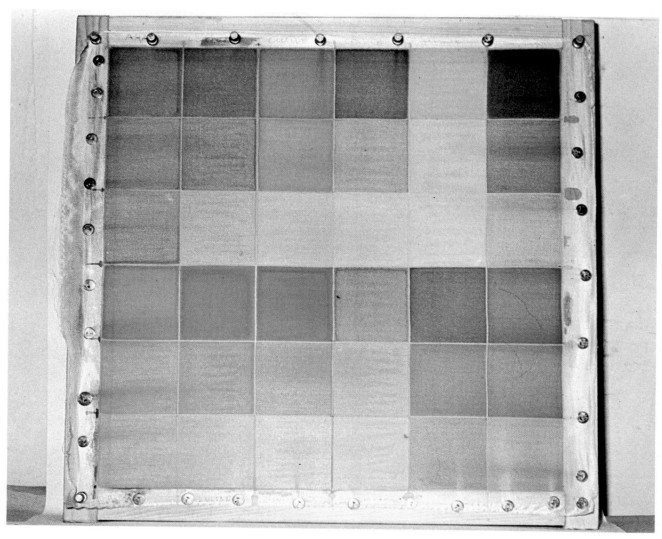

Colour-chart before fixing

Toxicity

These dyes are all produced by the chemical industry. The first two classes are based on aniline, a substance which is toxic when undiluted and which, although fairly harmless in solution, can nevertheless cause allergic reactions. The workplace must be well-ventilated when using alcohol to dilute the dyes.

Fixing

The designs created with these colouring agents remain highly fugitive until they are fixed. They must be kept out of the light and safe from splashes of water, which will leave indelible marks.

Fixing is achieved by prolonged steaming (see page 58); the colours then become brighter and will not fade or run so easily. Silks can be washed in warm soapy water.

All the finished pieces displayed in this book have been photographed after fixing.

Colour-chart after fixing

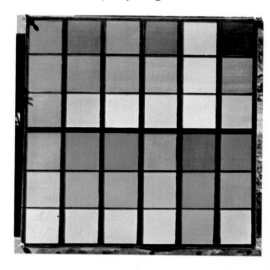

2. Colours which do not run

These are paints which remain on the surface of the fabric. If the silk is thin enough they will penetrate the fibres sufficiently for the design to appear on both sides, whereas with thick silks the reverse side of the design will not be as sharp.

These products are sold in various forms:

A. Pastes

Pastes are sold widely in craft-supply shops, usually as 'fabric paints'. These paints are alizarine-based, i.e. synthetic chemical products. The binding agent which gives them their smooth consistency is an emulsion of water, white spirit and an emulsifier. Generally the fixative is blended in by the manufacturer.

They can be mixed together and are diluted in water. A neutral base allows the colours to be toned down without affecting their consistency.

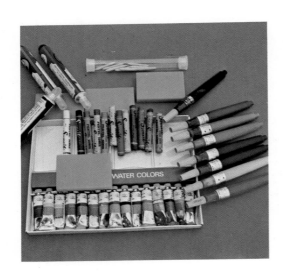

As these paints are transparent, they can be used only on white or light-coloured silks. One colour can be applied on top of another, provided dark covers light.

There is an opaque white which can be used either to make a colour opaque and to tone it down or to provide an undercoat for working on dark silks. The disadvantage is that the layer of white makes the silk slightly heavier.

B. Gouache

Dissolved in water, gouache is used on silk in the same way as it is used on paper. However, gouache will run on contact with water.

C. Fabric crayons

Some colours come in the form of wax crayons. A hot iron will melt the wax and the colours will then penetrate the silk fibres.

D. Ball-point and felt-tip pens

Special pens filled with fabric paints can be used to draw on silk just as on paper. They are very handy for minor alterations and fine detail. Ordinary pens are generally not suitable.

Fixing

These products can be fixed by contact with heat, usually by ironing both sides of the fabric with a hot iron. The colours will not then run or fade.

You can buy an anti-stain aerosol spray which protects decorated fabrics and is just the job for use on neckties. A quick wipe with a damp sponge removes stains without a trace.

You can see from this list that there is a large selection of products designed for decorating fabrics, especially silk; but each has its own specific uses. Thus, a colour which runs will be perfect for putting in a plain background but does not lend itself to drawing fine detail as well as does a non-running colour, and vice versa.

Similarly, the methods of application and the ways of mounting the silk differ according to the class of product used.

For these reasons we feel it most appropriate to devote one major chapter to colours which run and a second chapter to those which do not.

Decorative panel using the serti technique with gutta

1. Colours which run

Stretching frames

To achieve a successful design using any of these products, you need to have the silk perfectly evenly stretched before you start. Therefore a stretching frame is essential.

Several sorts of frame exist, their main distinguishing features being the way in which the silk is fixed in place and the system for maintaining the tension.

A. Frames using drawing-pins

These are the simplest frames. They must be built of wood which is soft enough to allow the drawing-pins to be pushed in easily, yet strong enough not to warp when under tension. Dry pine is ideal. They are easily home-made, being basically collapsible frames with sides which can be adapted in length to the standard dimensions of silk. There are two kinds, fixed-tension frames and adjustable-tension frames.

1. Fixed-tension frames

a) Frame for small silk squares (40 × 40 cm maximum)
The sides are simply slotted together to produce the required size of frame. The silk is secured on all four sides.

Advantages: quick and easy to assemble, lightweight.

Disadvantages: the joints tend to loosen with time, thus making the frame slack.

b) Frame for any size of silk
The sides of appropriate length are screwed together.

The silk is secured on all four sides.

Advantages: quick and easy to assemble, rigid joints. Possible to have sides long enough to stretch fairly large pieces of silk.

Disadvantages: the need to have a frame for each size of silk square.

Inherent disadvantages of this type of frame
It is sometimes helpful to pull the silk taut again in mid-design. This can be done only by removing and reinserting the drawing-pins, which marks the silk.

Fixed-tension frames
Frame for small silk squares
Frame for any size of silk

2. Adjustable-tension frames

This system allows the silk to be stretched taut again without unfastening it.

These frames are made of four slats of wood of the same thickness and length and with identical holes drilled in them.

The normal size is 3 × 5 × 120 cm, although an experiment with slats 2 cm thick and 140 cm long produced good results.

Each slat has one slot and holes every 10 cm. The photograph shows how to assemble them. Four wing-nuts keep the frame rigid.

The silk is secured on two sides only. It is pulled taut by moving outwards the slat mounted on the slots, and then fastening the two wing-nuts.

Advantages: it is easy to stretch the silk and adjust the tension.

Disadvantages: the frame is oversized for small squares. Securing the silk on two sides only means that the tension is not uniform in all directions.

This drawback can be overcome by using crocodile clips attached to elastic bands, as illustrated. In order for the clips to grip firmly without damaging the silk, fold a piece of adhesive tape around a match and stick it to both sides of the fabric edge.

Mounting the silk with crocodile clips

Mounting the silk on drawing-pin frames
In all cases the pins should be capable of being both firmly fixed and easily removed.

There is a choice of three types:
● drawing pins with a very strong point.
● architect's pins, which offer the advantage of three points to hold the silk and which can be easily removed with the small lever supplied in each box.

You should use these two types of pin whenever you intend to rule lines on the silk—when applying gutta, for example.

● American push-pins with a long point and an aluminium head, which means that they can be easily inserted and removed by hand. They are long-lasting but relatively expensive.

Mounting on fixed-tension frames
Start in the middle of one side. Stick a drawing-pin in approximately every 3 cm.

Next, stretch the silk along a side at right angles to the first.

Pin frame

Brushing the silk into place

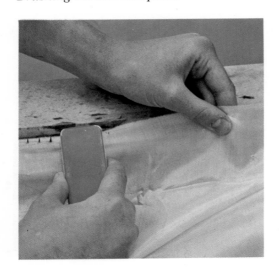

Then pull it taut diagonally and secure the third and fourth sides.

When the operation is complete the silk should be like a drumskin, with no sags or creases.

Mounting on adjustable-tension frames

Adjust the frame according to the size of the piece of silk to be stretched. Fasten one edge of the silk onto the fixed slat, starting in the middle. Apply a spot of glue to each corner of the silk and double up the drawing pins at the corners. Do the same on the adjustable slat. Pull the silk taut by sliding the adjustable slat outwards. Do this gently so as not to tear the silk. Where necessary, use the method described above to correct the tension.

B. Frames using pins

These are adjustable-tension frames. They have two slats each with two slots and a row of sharp pins at 1-cm intervals, and two other slats with holes and slots.

The silk is attached solely to the pins.

Progressively stretch the silk over the pins using a brush. *Be careful!* The pins are very sharp and can easily prick your fingers.

The stretching is done in the same way as with the previous frame, by sliding the movable slat outwards.

Advantages: perfectly uniform tension in all directions; easy to adjust.

Disadvantages: risk of injury from the pins; relatively expensive.

One recent development is a metal frame which holds the silk in place magnetically. Because it leaves no marks on the silk it is the ideal frame. However, it is currently very expensive, and hard to find.

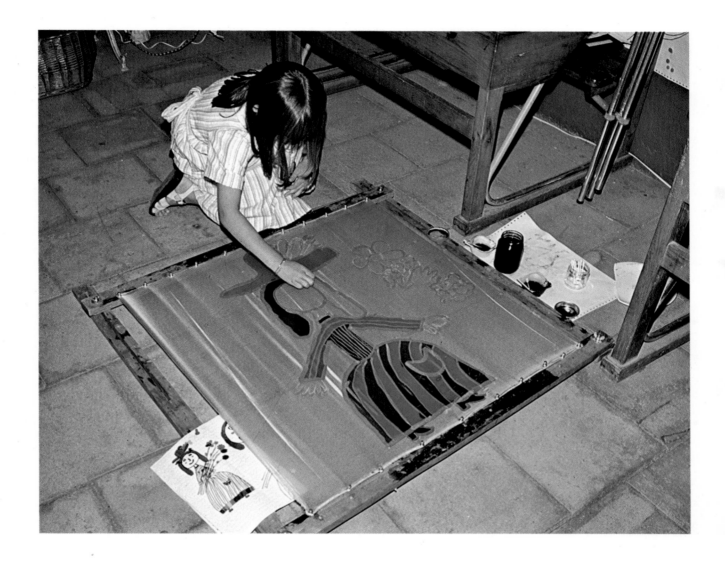

The work surface

With colours which run, always work on a flat surface.

You can set up your frame on a suitably sized table or on trestles. Two trestles are generally enough, but long frames will require a third to prevent sagging, which upsets the tension. As you will be working standing up, you should avoid having to bend forward too much, which is very tiring. Find the working height which suits you by raising your table or trestles on bricks or old telephone directories. Children can work very well on the floor. To avoid the chore of having to clean up, cover the floor and the work surface with newspaper or a sheet of plastic.

Applicators

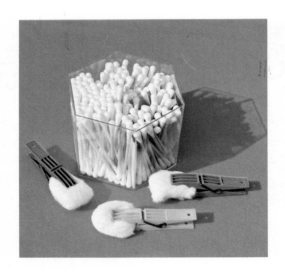

Most importantly, these should be capable of holding enough paint to cover quite a large area without needing constant refilling.

The cheapest and most practical material is cotton wool. For large areas use a tightly-rolled ball of cotton wool gripped in a plastic clothes peg.

For small areas use cotton-buds.

Use a different applicator for each colour, and throw them away after use.

Instead of cotton pads you can use refillable pens or brushes. Again, remember, one pen for each colour.

Wash brushes
With their fine tip and large reserve of paint they are the ideal tools for both large and small surfaces.

Their one great drawback is their price, which means that you are unlikely to be able to afford a brush for every colour. Therefore they have to be washed in soapy water at each colour change. Rinse carefully and then leave them to dry, bristles uppermost, before re-using.

We ourselves use only cotton buds and pads together with a few fine brushes for very small areas.

Cotton buds and pads
Felt-tip pens and reservoir brushes
Wash brushes

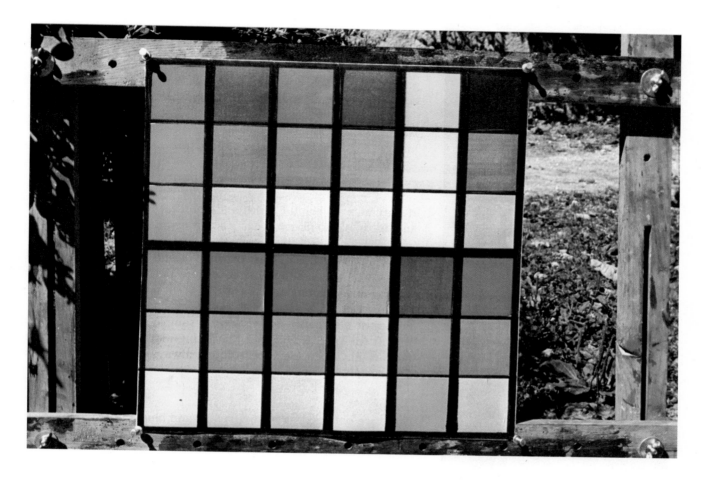

Colour effects

Colour-chart after fixing

The choice of colours

Since such a wide range of colours is commercially available, a choice has to be made.

We suggest here a selection from among the 'professional' products. It is a deliberately limited range of only twelve shades, since the scope for blending and diluting is so wide that your twelve basic colours will allow you to create an almost limitless number of hues.

A special section is devoted to blending greens and greys.

Manufacturers often give their products highly fanciful names. A shade of turquoise may be called macaw by one maker and Chinese blue by another. That is why we have not given a name to the shades we have selected. You need simply match them up with the labels of your chosen supplier.

The colour-chart above shows each paint first undiluted then diluted with the water-alcohol mixture in the ratios 1 to 3 and 1 to 6. All the intermediate ratios are likewise possible.

Greens and greys

N.B. As a rule, when you make up a colour you must always gauge in advance how much you will need for the area to be covered. It is better to have a little too much than not enough.

As a guide, on a fine habutai you need about one teaspoonful of mixture to cover 1000 square centimetres.

A thicker silk requires a greater volume of colour.

It may also be helpful to keep a record of the quantities used in any one blend so that you can make it up at another time.

Prepare your blends in glass or white plastic containers. Coloured plastic would not allow you to ensure that you get exactly the shade you are aiming at.

You must also carry out tests on a sample strip of silk to judge how it will look. Remember that fixing makes the colours much more vivid. When blending colours, always pour the lighter one into the container first.

Greens
These are obtained by mixing yellow and blue, but red and brown can also be added.

Take half as much yellow as is necessary for the surface-area to be covered, adding the blue with an eye-dropper and stirring with a glass rod. When you have the required shade, add some of it to the water-alcohol mixture.

Test it on a spare piece of silk and assess the shade against a white background when dry.

The addition of a few drops of red or brown will give the green extra warmth.

The basic shade is now ready. It can be diluted to obtain a lighter hue.

Greys
Pour out an amount of water-alcohol mixture sufficient for the area to be covered.

Darken this colourless base by adding black to it drop by drop. When it appears dark enough, test it as you did the green.

Adding just black will give a 'hollow' grey. To give it more body it is advisable to add a few drops of colour. This can yield the most striking coloured greys.

Subtle colours

When a design is finished it sometimes looks too garish with over-bright colours. There are two possible remedies.

Clean water wash
Quickly dipping your silk in at least two litres of water will release some of the dye and soften the colours. Dry the silk on a line, avoiding runs.

Dyeing
Prepare a dye bath with water and a little dash of blue, brown, violet or black, depending on the colours of the design, and dip your silk quickly in it. Dry as before.

Removing colours

Sometimes you may be totally dissatisfied with a design. There is a way of recovering the silk by soaking it in a cleansing bath. The proportions of cleanser and water are shown on the packet. Rinsing gives you an off-white silk which can be decorated once again.

Keeping the products

Undiluted and unmixed products keep very well in tightly-sealed glass containers, as mentioned earlier.

Blended colours can occasionally settle and must be filtered before re-use.

To avoid having a host of jars containing different mixtures, simply equip yourself with five large jars into which you can pour all your leftover colours — that is, one each for the blues, browns, greens, reds and violets. These mixtures will be very useful as a base for muted colours to enhance the brighter tones of a pattern.

Special effects

Two techniques allow you to avoid the monotony of plain surfaces.

1. Cooking salt

If some perfectly dry crystals of cooking salt are sprinkled on a freshly painted, still-damp colour, you will see the water and alcohol being rapidly absorbed by the salt and some of the colour migrating to the edge of the affected patches.

The swirls created during the absorption of the liquid by the salt yield unpredictable but always very striking designs.

The effects can, however, be controlled by placing the salt according to a set pattern rather than scattering it at random.

Effect of the cooking salt after two minutes

Salt pattern after fixing

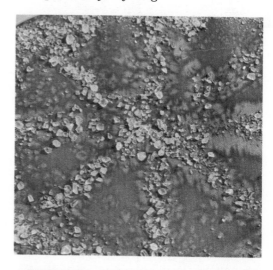

Decorative panel
Cooking salt and discolouring

N.B. When a design is to be composed of plain areas and areas treated with salt, always start with the plain areas and let them dry properly before moving on to the areas to be treated. The reverse order is not practicable because there is always one salt crystal that falls in the wrong place and causes a stain where it shouldn't.

Remove the salt when the colours are completely dry.

Pattern made by discolouring

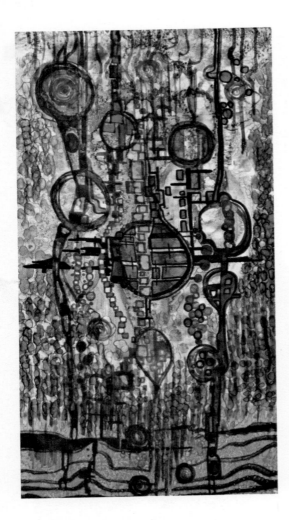

Detail

Facing page: *special effects obtained with cooking salt*

2. Alcohol

If a drop of water–alcohol mixture accidentally falls on a coloured surface, you will see that it spreads, pushing back the colour pigments towards its outer edge. This peculiarity can be exploited to bring variety to a plain surface. You simply dab the surface with a cotton-bud soaked in pure alcohol.

Cooking salt and alcohol are a godsend for the less dextrous designer, enabling a mistake to be turned to a decorative advantage.

But be careful not to overdo it!

Background colours

Silk treated for decoration should be white. In some cases it is easier to fill in the whole surface with a coloured background before starting on the design proper.

This background may be plain or shade off into white or from one colour into another.

In every case the secret of success is in the speed of execution.

A plain background

First method
This entails dyeing the whole of the fabric by soaking it in a dye bath. It is advisable to wear a pair of protective rubber gloves for this job.

Prepare a bath containing twice the amount of dyestuff necessary for covering the surface by the cotton pad method.

Completely immerse the fabric in the bath for several seconds, squeeze it and hang it up to dry.

Second method
Prepare enough colour to cover the entire surface of the fabric.

Prepare two cotton pads and grip them in clothes-pegs.

Soak the first pad in the dye until it is completely saturated, then put the other pad in the dye. Using the first pad, apply the colour to the surface of the silk, which should be properly stretched width-wise.

When the first pad starts to run out of colour, put it to soak again and switch to the second pad, which by then will be saturated. Use the two pads in turn until the surface is entirely covered.

A gradated background

Shading from a colour to white
Prepare two containers and two cotton pads, one set for the water—alcohol mixture, the other for the colour.

Wet the bottom two-thirds of the fabric with the water—alcohol mixture.

Apply the colour, moving from the dry part towards the wet part.

When the colour reaches the wet part it will be diluted by the colourless mixture and will become progressively lighter. Stop applying colour two-thirds of the way down.

With the pad soaked in the colourless mixture, start from the blank area and work two-thirds of the way up the fabric.

Shading from one colour to another
Let us take blue shading into green, for example.

Prepare three containers and three cotton pads – one set for the blue, another for the green, and another for a mixture of equal parts of blue and green. Divide the surface into three zones of about one-third each. Start with the blue, then continue with the mixture, overlapping the two. Finish off with the green, overlapping again.

Work up again from the green to the blue with the green pad but without re-soaking it.

N.B. All these operations must be carried out rapidly and must be completed before any one of the colours has time to dry. If necessary, ask a friend to help with the gradation.

An unsuccessful gradation will have rings and stripes which are darker than the surrounding area. It is virtually impossible to remove them.

Note. It is very easy to achieve good gradations by using one or two spray guns to apply the colours, but it is a very costly method.

Pink cushion
Coloured serti
Plain areas

Techniques for using colours that run

1. Direct painting

A. White background

Colours that run can be applied to silk using cotton-buds, brushes, or felt-tip pens.

In all cases, the designs will be blurred because of the penetration of the dyestuff through the fibres.

A number of trial runs will be necessary to master this technique completely.

You will notice, for example, that two adjacent colours are separated by a darker line when they dry; and that two colours applied on top of each other give a compound shade with a darker line at the outer edge.

A good exercise is to create tartan designs using three colours — blue, green and red, for example. Vary the thickness of the lines as well as the gaps between them. You will then be able to see how much the colours run and the effect of colours applied on top of each other.

Direct painting on coloured backgrounds

B. Coloured background

There are two possible cases:

Non-fixed coloured background
The design can be made either by mottling with undiluted alcohol, or by applying colours on top of each other.

In both cases, the lines are blurred and the patches of colour bordered by a dark ring, as happens with a white background.

Fixed coloured background
Mottling becomes impossible and layered colours blend only as an optical illusion. The paints cannot run together any longer.

A fixed coloured silk reduces the running of the colours, so giving much neater designs.

Needless to say, the finished work must be fixed.

Treatment of the silk to prevent the paints from running

First method
Dissolve 250 g of cooking salt in a litre of warm water. After an hour, filter the solution through a filter paper to remove the undissolved grains of salt.

Soak the silk in this salt bath and dry it on a line.

Lampshade by direct painting

Second method

Make a mixture of 5% gutta and 95% white spirit. Apply this solution to the stretched silk with a brush. Leave it to dry.

N.B. Be careful not to work near a naked flame, and leave the window open during the application of the solution and the drying.

This technique of painting on silk treated to avoid running, is especially useful for graphics work. Indeed, it is not recommended for large areas since the brush strokes would be visible and the result, if you are not very skilful, would be disappointing.

2. Wax resist

Hot wax applied on silk penetrates the fibres and prevents them from being dyed. This process forms the basis of an extremely old technique of decorating silk—batik.

The technique we suggest in this book is derived from batik and is called *imitation batik*. As this name is a bit limiting and fairly derogatory, we have preferred to call it *wax resist*.

It is a very simple technique which gives outstanding results. The basic principle, as with traditional batik, is to protect a white or coloured area with a coat of hot wax. The dye, instead of being applied by soaking, is painted on the silk which is stretched on a frame. Although this process avoids removing the silk from the frame each time a dye is to be applied, it does not naturally lend itself to cracking in the areas coated with wax. It is thus necessary to create cracks once the painting is finished, hence the name imitation batik.

A. The wax

This is a mixture of paraffin wax and beeswax. The richer the mixture in paraffin wax, the lower its melting-point.

By experimenting with various proportions of these two products, you can obtain either a soft drawing wax, rich in beeswax, with which you can draw neatly without any cracks, or a brittle wax, rich in paraffin wax, with which you can obtain the veinings typical of batik.

Drawing wax

This is made of 40% beeswax and 60% paraffin wax by weight.

Paraffin wax is sold as household candles or in flakes or blocks from craft shops or candlemakers' suppliers. Beeswax is usually sold in blocks and is more expensive. The yellow colour of beeswax does not affect the silk. A mixture in powder form is sold in craft shops as 'Batik wax' and is very convenient.

Wax-resist without cerné

Wax-resist with cerné and crackings

Brittle wax
This is made of 30% beeswax and 70% paraffin wax.

Preparing the mixtures
The components are melted together in an aluminium container. To avoid any risk of fire, it is best not to use a naked flame, unless the mixture is melted using a double pan. Use the lowest heat at which the wax will melt completely.

The ideal is to use an electric ring with a thermostat which allows the mixture to be melted directly in the aluminium pan.

Heating must be stopped at once if a trace of smoke can be seen—firstly because it smells bad, but mainly because the fumes of hot wax are highly flammable.

Drawing with a brush

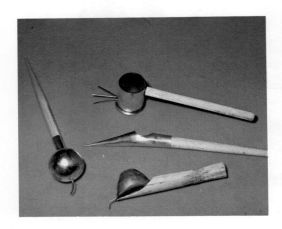

Tjantings

Tjap

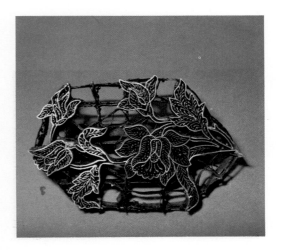

B. Drawing with wax

1. Using a brush

This is the simplest technique, but the thickness of the lines is not regular, and brushes are quickly damaged by the hot wax.

On the other hand, a brush allows greater freedom in drawing, avoiding the monotony of an outline which is too sharply defined.

2. Using a tjanting

The tjanting is a copper bowl mounted on a handle, which has a very fine spout from which the wax is poured. There are several types available, but, the one most commonly found in shops is bowl-shaped and difficult to use.

The advantage of using a tjanting is that it gives a continuous and even line. Good ones are very simple to use:

(a) dip the tjanting into the hot wax, and leave it for a few seconds to bring the copper to the temperature of the wax.

(b) close the end of the spout with a cotton pad (or a tissue) and hold the tjanting above the silk.

(c) remove the cotton pad and outline the drawing with the wax which flows from the tjanting.

(d) when the tjanting is not in contact with the silk, close the end of the spout immediately to avoid misplaced wax blobs.

3. Using the Javanese tjap

The tjap is a printing block made of copper strips soldered together to form a motif.

Immerse the tjap into the hot wax and leave it for at least three minutes to adapt to the temperature. Then take it out, let it drip and apply it to the silk, pressing hard.

To facilitate printing, the silk should be placed on a flat, unbending surface. You can use a sheet of hardboard, covered with tracing-paper or transparent paper such as glassine.

Applying wax with a tjanting. The piece of paper is used to catch the drops of wax

C. Wax resists and designs

The pattern
Every time you undertake to paint a large design, it is essential to draw a full-size pattern on a sheet of paper.

There are two methods which make it easy to follow the outline of the pattern.

1. See-through method
The pattern, drawn with a black felt-tip pen, is placed under the frame, and the outline can thus be followed through the silk. The pattern should not be in contact with the silk.

The ideal method is to place a pane of glass on two trestles, lay the pattern on the pane, and then position the frame above it.

A lamp placed underneath the pane should enable you to follow the design easily through the silk.

2. Rough outline
A rough outline of the pattern can be traced in pencil directly on the silk by transferring the drawing through the silk. Fine details should be left out.

N.B. In all cases, do not feel you have to stick to your pattern. It is better to have a line slightly different from your original pattern than one which follows it but which is shaky and uneven.

Coloured pattern and full-size design using the see-through method

Tjap printing – an aspect of cerné

Wax-resist with cerné

The design

1. Designs with cerné
Cerné work means using a continuous wax line which encloses areas to be painted. Serti, which will be dealt with later on, uses the cerné technique, but not the hot wax.

If the original colour of the silk is white, the cerné lines will be white. On the other hand, if the fabric is coloured, the lines will be of the same colour.

First, trace with drawing wax around any area which is going to remain the colour of the silk. (In the lamp-shade on the left, this means all the area around the main design.)

Then trace the fine lines which will enclose the coloured areas on the main design. Apply the colours, starting with the lighter ones, to the enclosed areas. Which applicator you use depends upon the size of the area to be covered: it can be a cotton-bud, a brush, a felt-tip pen, or a cotton pad.

Leave the paint to dry. Drying can be speeded up using a hair-drier on a cool setting.

The first application of dye can be followed by many others. All you have to do is protect with the wax the areas you want to keep. Then you can apply another colour to the wax-free areas.

The further you progress with the painting, the darker the shades obtained by applying one colour on top of another.

It is essential to wait for the paint to dry completely before applying another coat of hot wax.

2. Designs without cerné

This method needs to be thought out more thoroughly than the previous one. Moreover, the different stages are completely separate.

Let's choose a design in white, black and pink.

To start with, protect (with the drawing wax) the areas you want to remain white.

Apply the pink colour over the whole surface and leave it to dry.

Protect the pink with a coat of wax. Apply the black to the unwaxed areas.

Your painting is finished. With this kind of design where the dyes are applied on top of each other, you must plan in advance to apply them in the correct order.

As a rule, it is best to proceed from light to dark. To appreciate the effect, look at your design by holding it up to the light.

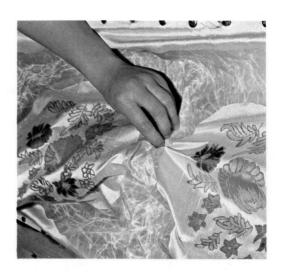

Cracking the wax

Crackings are not compulsory but they enable the different parts of the design to be linked together and give your painting a certain unity.

Once the dyes have been applied and the silk is perfectly dry, cover the whole fabric with brittle wax, using a large brush.

N.B. Your wax must be hot when applied if you do not want to see it flake away when cracking.

Leave it to harden.

Slacken the tension of the silk or remove it from the frame and crumple it in your hands to crack the wax.

You can also obtain cracking in one direction only by folding the silk. Or you can crack the wax in some parts of the fabric and not in others.

When the cracks are made, place the silk on a sheet of kraft paper or stretch it again on the frame. Then, using a cotton-pad soaked in a dark colour matching the rest of the painting, rub the surface of the silk.

The colour penetrates the cracks and dyes them.

Leave it to dry.

Removing the wax

The wax is removed by ironing the silk between two sheets of paper. Any absorbent paper is suitable – even newspaper, provided it has not just been printed.

The process must be repeated until the last visible traces of wax have been removed. Any remaining wax will disappear during fixing.

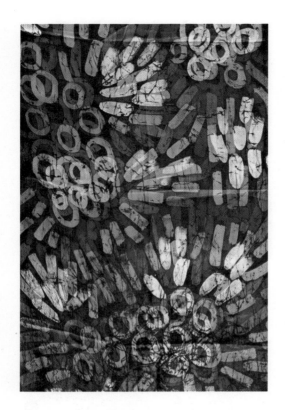

Celine's scarf

Faults and corrections

The main problem when applying the wax is drops falling in the wrong place. It is impossible to remove them, but they can be incorporated into the design so that they are no longer noticeable.

Controlled splashing of hot wax can give original designs. But be careful not to splash it all over. Make sure the walls and the floor of the workplace are protected with newspaper or kraft paper.

Another problem that can occur when applying the dye is the ring stain. Like the wax blob, this is impossible to remove. It happens when applying a new colour on top of an already dry colour.

It is possible to avoid it when the pattern is designed: reduce the size of the areas to be dyed by dividing them up with wax lines.

These rings can be toned down by dabbing the surface with a cotton bud soaked in undiluted alcohol.

In all cases, they will be nearly invisible when all the cracks are dyed.

To sum up, one can say that wax-resist is ideal for beginners. It requires the least precision, as the technique itself allows mistakes to be turned into creative designs.

1. Applying the colours
2. Detail using felt-tip pens
3. Protecting the petals with wax to avoid smudges when the dyestuffs are applied to the background
4. Colouring the background and applying cooking salt
5. Applying wax to the centre of the flower to obtain crackings to be coloured later
6. Removing the cooking salt
7. Cracking the centre of the flower
8. Removing the wax with a hot iron after colouring the crackings

1

2

3

4

5

6

7

8

Detail of coloured gutta serti

Scarf
Clear gutta serti

3. Gutta and serti

Gutta

"Gutta-percha – a white rubber substance derived from the coagulated milky latex of (certain tropical) trees"—*Collins English Dictionary*.

Gutta is commercially available in the form of a thick, colourless, slightly opalescent liquid which gives, when dry, a soft and elastic substance sticking to the fabric to which it has been applied.

Applied in thin coats on a stretched piece of silk, gutta penetrates the fibres and closes the mesh, making it waterproof.

An easy-to-use, water-based 'gutta' has recently come on the market.

Serti

Serti is the technique of forming designs using gutta to separate the colours. It is the waterproof property of gutta which is used to prevent the colours from running through the silk.

A thin line of gutta on the silk creates a real barrier that dyes cannot penetrate. It is thus possible with gutta to achieve partitioned designs, similar to stained-glass windows. The gutta acts like the lead strips between which are set the pieces of coloured glass composing the stained-glass window. This, then, is serti.

Although the theory sounds simple, in practice using gutta sometimes poses technical problems which may be hard to overcome. First of all there is its *consistency* at the moment of application, which determines how effectively it penetrates the silk and prevents the dyes running. Then there are the different methods of application, which determine the sharpness of the serti line.

Consistency of the gutta
It is rare to find ready-to-use gutta in the shops. Because gutta has to be diluted in refined petrol or white spirit—both very volatile—it tends to thicken with time, even if kept in a tightly closed container. A gutta which is too thick is no use for serti.

Indeed, if the product is too thick, it cannot penetrate the silk and forms a barrier without foundations under which the dyes can easily run. Therefore, gutta must be diluted with a solvent such as white spirit, which can be found in hardware shops.

But be careful! Here again, to overdo it is a mistake. An over-diluted gutta penetrates the fibres easily, but it will not be thick enough to block the mesh and the dyes will run just the same.

So what *is* the right consistency?

There is no precise specification. As a rule, an effective gutta should have the consistency of runny honey and should dry within ten minutes of application.

Dilution of the gutta
Gutta should be diluted just before use.

Place the gutta in a glass container, and add the white spirit drop by drop, stirring continuously with a wooden or glass rod.

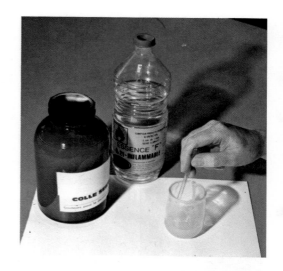

To check the consistency of the gutta, take the stick out of the container. A trickle of gutta should run from the stick into the pot.

A drop of gutta pressed between two fingers should, when you slowly open out your fingers, form a thread 3 cm long before breaking.

Your gutta is now ready for use. Do not wait if you do not want evaporation to ruin your careful preparations.

Appearance of the gutta
Colourless gutta. The area of the silk to which the gutta is to be applied remains undyed. This area will be the original colour of the fabric, in most cases white.

When the dyes used are very pale, it is sometimes difficult to make out the line of the serti. Overcome this by colouring the gutta to obtain a coloured serti.

Coloured gutta. The dyestuffs to use are thick printing-ink, glycerophthalic glass-stain, or any paint or coloured varnish soluble in white spirit.

The preparation of the mixture is as follows: Take a small quantity of dyestuff and mix it up with white spirit until it is completely dissolved. Use this mixture to dilute the gutta to the right consistency.

CAUTION! Even after being fixed, the dyestuff used to colour the gutta does not resist dry-cleaning. The fabric should only be washed in lukewarm water with soap.

Applying the gutta
The aim is to apply a cordon of gutta to prevent the dyestuff penetrating the silk and so to create a partitioned design.

Gutta is applied using a pipette or a cone.

The pipette. This is the simplest method, ideal for beginners. It is made of a flexible plastic container with a screw-on cap and sealed plastic spout with its own small cap.

The spout should be pierced with as fine a needle as possible.

To fill the pipette, use a paper funnel. When the pipette is full,

2

3

5

7

screw on the cap and leave the small cap on the spout to avoid evaporation.

To have a perfectly calibrated hole, cover the spout with an architect's pen. These come in a variety of sizes, the most useful being 0.8, 1.2, 1.5 and 2. They should be cleaned in white spirit after use.

The cone. This is the professional way. It lends itself to drawing fine detail, and gives greater flexibility in outlining the serti, but it is difficult to make.

The best materials to use are florist's transparent paper (glassine or similar), greaseproof paper, tracing paper; and some adhesive tape to stick the cone together.

To make a good cone, follow the instructions below.
1) Cut out a rectangle from a sheet of paper (about 15 cm × 25 cm), and mark the middle of its length by creasing it gently.
2) Cut out a 10° triangle with the crease at the apex.
3) Bend the paper without folding it and roll it to form a cone.
4) Check the size of the hole (which should be as small as possible) by looking through the inside of the cone.
5) Secure the tip of the cone using adhesive tape.
6) Seal the cone with adhesive tape around and along the outside.
7) Half fill the cone with gutta. Place your cone above a container to catch the gutta flowing through the spout.
8) Get rid of the air by flattening the cone between two fingers at the level of the gutta and by sliding two fingers of the other hand upwards, squeezing the cone.
9) Using scissors, straighten the top of the cone.
10) Close it by rolling it like a tube of toothpaste.
11) Use adhesive tape to make it airtight – now your cone is ready for use.

8

Test applications

Try it on a sheet of paper first.

The pipette is held like a fountain-pen, pressing it slightly between the fingers to force out the gutta.

If your pipette is fitted with a nib, it should be held in an upright position.

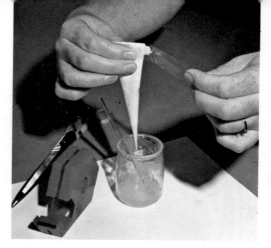

The pipette must be moved steadily. Speed plays an essential part in the thickness of the gutta trail.

When used on fabric, the pipette must exert a slight pressure on the silk to make the gutta penetrate the fibres.

The cone is held as illustrated. Pressure is exerted at the top of the cone.

A slight scratching should be heard when the spout of the cone rubs against the silk.

Careful! Always pull the cone. Do not push it forward, for the tip may catch in the fabric, which would result in an uneven line.

Beginners should not try to draw a precise design, but should endeavour to master the technique first. For this, draw rectangles, squares, circles, ovals, etc. The line must be continuous.

N.B. When you start a line of gutta, a blob very often appears. To avoid this, start your line on a piece of thin paper placed on the silk.

On thicker fabrics, such as wild silk, doupion and noile, a thicker line should be drawn. For this, the hole of the spout of the cone or the pipette should be larger and the pressure exerted stronger. The cone or pipette should also be moved more slowly.

If, despite all these precautions, the line of gutta does not stop the dyestuff, another line of gutta should be applied on the back of the fabric.

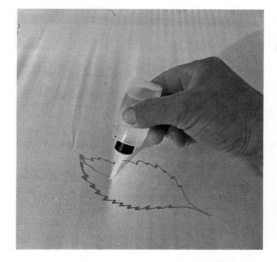

Straight lines can be drawn using a ruler. Use a flat ruler with a bevel to avoid smudges of gutta along the ruler edge.

There are also various ways of drawing circles. Cardboard stencils can be used, but because you cannot draw a complete circle with them in one go, a few touches have to be added (by hand), and these show.

Or you can make your own 'compasses', according to the size of the circles. These are made out of a rigid cardboard strip which can revolve around a push pin or drawing-pin.

Holes pierced along the strip enable you to insert the spout of the pipette vertically. The best results are obtained with a pipette fitted with a nib.

Concentric circles can be drawn in this way, but you can also draw circles which intersect by moving the pin around which the cardboard strip turns.

To draw circles in one go, use a perforated strip of cardboard

Scarf
Clear gutta serti

The cardboard strip should not touch the silk or it will rub against the gutta. So fold back the strip 5 mm from the end. Three cardboard washers should be threaded through the push pin to raise the strip.

Finally, to insert the push pin, the stretched fabric should be placed 5 mm above a piece of plywood, covered with a sheet of smooth drawing paper.

This 5-mm space is just enough for the fabric and the paper to touch when you draw with the pipette, but the elasticity of the stretched silk should prevent the fabric from sticking to the paper. Fabric and paper should not remain in contact or smudges will result.

Judging the results

1. The gutta is not dry after ten minutes
Causes: 1. gutta too thick.
              2. line of gutta too thick.
Consequences: the gutta will remain sticky even after being fixed.
Remedy: the gutta should be removed either before applying the dyestuffs, or after fixing.

In order to do this, soak the silk in some white spirit until the gutta has completely disappeared. Rinse the silk in clean white spirit, since traces of gutta would affect penetration of the dyestuffs.

Do this outdoors or in a well-ventilated room.

N.B. If the gutta is coloured, the dye will be removed by the white spirit.

If this process has been carried out before applying the dyestuff, the silk will be blank. If it has been carried out after fixing, the line of gutta will be the same colour as the silk.

2. Smudges or spots
Causes: 1. you accidentally touched the gutta while it was wet.
              2. the pipette or the cone dripped.
              3. the pattern was in contact with the silk.
Prevention: 1. start the design as if you were writing a letter at the top left-hand corner and moving from left to right (from right to left for left-handed people).
              2. hold a piece of paper under the spout of the pipette or the cone whilst it is moving above the silk.
              3. make sure the pattern is about 1 cm from the silk.
Remedies: 1. remove the gutta by rubbing on one side with a cotton pad soaked in white spirit, and on the other side with a dry cotton pad.
              2. repeat the process, changing cotton pads until the gutta is completely removed.

Applying dyestuffs

As we mentioned at the beginning of the book, speed is an advantage in the decoration of silk, but this does not mean that you must rush into things without thinking beforehand.

Light colours should always be applied first.

For small areas, cotton-buds, fine brushes, or refillable felt pens with fine tips should be used.

For large areas, it is best to use cotton pads, wash-brushes or brushes with a reservoir.

Always start applying the dyestuff from the centre of the area to be painted, and let the dye run up to the line of gutta.

For backgrounds, it may be useful to work in pairs in order to avoid the rings which appear when painting over a coloured area which has already dried.

Avoid using too much dyestuff. This results in drops running through the silk and staining your worktable, or in patchy colours, or even in dye crossing the gutta barrier.

Faults due to the gutta

When you apply the dyestuff, it penetrates the serti.
Causes: 1. the line of gutta is not continuous and the dye runs through the gaps.
             2. the gutta is too thick and the dyestuff runs underneath the line of gutta.
             3. the gutta is too dilute (runny) and has not blocked the mesh.
             4. the gutta is adequate but has failed to penetrate a thick fabric.
Remedies: 1. close the gaps with touches of gutta.
             2. apply some more gutta on the inside of the line if it is too thin, or on the back if the gutta has not penetrated all the way through.

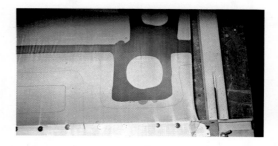

Dyestuff running through the serti

Removing smudges with cotton-buds soaked in undiluted alcohol after restoring the serti

Faults due to the dyestuffs

Actually it is not so much the dyestuffs which are at fault as the way they have been applied.
Causes: 1. the application of the colours has not been carried out properly and has run over the line of gutta.
             2. too much dyestuff has been applied.
Remedy: After correcting the serti if need be, remove the smudges of dyestuff with a cotton bud soaked in undiluted alcohol. This is a very long process and rings are likely to appear where a new colour is applied. This risk is minimised if you started with light colours.

In this case, cooking salt or other decoloration techniques can be used (see pages 19 and 20), but it is a makeshift remedy.

Serti designs

1. The choice of the motif

Any motifs can be drawn using the serti technique, but they should be adapted to the potential of the process.

As a rule, try to make it as simple as possible, avoiding elaborate detail and over-large 'plain' areas. In fact, it is as difficult to draw fine details with gutta as it is to obtain uniform shades when painting large areas with irregular outlines.

To start with, use geometric figures: stripes of different width, simple interlinked patterns, then curves and rounded enclosed areas. Figurative motifs should be tried later.

It may be interesting to get some inspiration for designs from abstract paintings – but without copying them.

2. The pattern

The graphics
The ideal is first to make a small-scale pattern, and then a full-scale outline to be used for applying the gutta by the see-through method or by transfer with a pencil.

The choice of colours
This must be thought out carefully and not decided at random.

It is best to prepare all the necessary shades of colour before starting work.

The original design can be coloured with these colours and the corresponding areas on the full-size drawing numbered to avoid any mistakes.

The choice of colours is a personal matter but you must keep in mind that a balanced painting must have both calm areas with subtle colours, and livelier areas with brighter colours to attract the eye.

Since silk is a very rich fabric, the colour should emphasise its qualities but not kill them. The most successful designs are often the most understated ones. A painting in several shades of the same colour is one way of achieving this subdued effect.

3. Creating the design

If you are using the see-through method, your pattern should be placed underneath the fabric, near enough to be seen properly but without touching the silk. One centimetre is a reasonable gap.

In order to do this, pin your pattern onto two wooden sticks and slide it underneath the fabric. Resting on the cross-members of the frame, the sticks will keep the pattern in position.

Circles and spirals drawn in one go with gutta (see pages 37–38)

Positioning the pattern for design by the see-through method

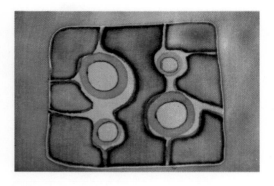

Retouching

Clear serti on a coloured background and painting in shades of one colour

Scarf with birds

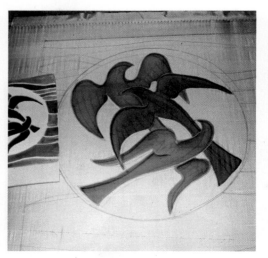

A piece of plywood can also be used, but it is necessary to have several pieces of various sizes to match the dimensions of the pieces of silk to be painted.

When you are drawing directly on silk, make sure your fabric is placed on a hard, smooth surface – such as plywood, for example – and do not draw with a pen which is too hard or too sharp or you will tear the silk.

Now you have only to apply the gutta and afterwards the colours.

The decoration is over, and you can now proceed to the last stage: fixing the dyestuffs (see page 58).

However, it may be that the result obtained does not live up to your expectations. It is still possible to improve it.

Retouching
To enliven an area which is too empty, lines of gutta and a pattern using shades of one colour are two satisfactory solutions.

Making colours more subtle
See page 18 and follow the instructions given.

Making colours more vivid
As already mentioned, colours are made much more vivid by the fixing process. Therefore, it is best to wait until the end before making any accurate judgement, at least when you are a beginner.

It *is* possible to make colours more vivid, but only in small areas because in larger areas there is a risk of ring stains.

The whole surface must be covered with a slightly darker colour than the first one. Finish off by matching the shades using a dry cotton bud.

Scarf with birds

Colourless gutta and cracking wax

This scarf is made from moussedoup, a shimmering fabric which makes blues catch the light like a butterfly's wings.

The full-size pattern taped on a sheet of plywood is placed about 1 cm underneath the silk. The design can be seen clearly through the fabric.

The dyes are ready for use, and a small-scale pattern will enable you to apply them without error.

The trailing of the serti using colourless gutta is done with a cone made of suitable paper (see page 36). Note how the cone is held.

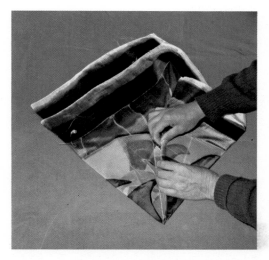

The birds are painted in. Note the shading of the colours, obtained by painting the silk with the water–alcohol mixture using a brush soaked in paint and a cotton bud which is simply moistened.

The dyestuffs are applied to the background. Each strip is gradually shaded from pink to dark blue. The background is now finished.

You can see that the white of the circle contrasts too sharply with the other colours of the scarf, so it is necessary to soften the contrast.

A wax-cracking effect is going to be used.

For this, coat the white of the circle and the blue edge of the scarf with hot wax.

When the wax has cooled down, remove the scarf from the frame.

The radiating cracks are obtained by folding the silk along the radius of the circle. The edges are just crumpled.

Then the silk is stretched again on the frame.

The edges of the circle, the outlines of the birds and the inner edges of the square are protected by a line of wax.

Pink, then blue, is applied over the cracks with a cotton bud.

Once the dyestuffs are completely dry, the wax is removed using a hot iron.

The decoration of the scarf is now finished and only needs to be fixed.

Roll the scarf in an absorbent paper (e.g. lining paper). Do not forget to roll the paper a few more times after wrapping the scarf completely.

Scarf with birds

Fixing in a pressure cooker

Removing the gutta after fixing in a bath of white spirit

Seal the roll at both ends and along its whole length using adhesive tape, then flatten and roll it into a snail shape.

Place the roll in the basket of the pressure-cooker and add about 2 cm of water.

Do not forget to place a trivet at the bottom of the pressure-cooker to prevent the basket from touching the water.

After placing a piece of aluminium foil folded in half on the roll, so that the condensation dripping from the lid does not wet the paper, place the basket in the pressure-cooker.

Close the lid and maintain pressure for 45 minutes.

Once the pressure-cooker has cooled down, open the lid, take out the roll and unfurl it.

You will find that the gutta sticks to the paper. To remove it, soak the scarf in a jar containing some white spirit, and leave it, lid closed, for a few minutes, shaking it continuously.

Then take out the scarf and let the white spirit evaporate. *CAREFUL!* This should be done outdoors or indoors with all the windows open.

You will note that the creases in the silk can still be seen clearly. To remove them, soak the silk in water and iron it whilst still wet.

1. Applying coloured gutta with a pipette fitted with a nib
2. Colouring
3. Splashing colours on the background using a nailbrush

The Queen of Hearts

Decorative panel
Coloured gutta

To make this panel, quite a thick fabric is used, such as tussore.

The pattern, taped on to a sheet of plywood, is placed in contact with the silk so that the design can be traced in pencil.

After removing the sheet of plywood, the design is drawn again with black-coloured gutta using a pipette fitted with a nib.

A piece of paper is used to prevent any spots of gutta from dripping when the pipette is moved over the silk.

Straight lines are drawn with a ruler.

When using a ruler, make sure your silk is perfectly taut. The lateral tension is maintained by crocodile clips (see p. 13).

The small areas are painted with a small, fine brush. A cotton bud is used for larger areas with simple outlines.

Touches of coloured gutta are used to emphasise details.

The flecked background is made by splashing on the dyestuff with a nailbrush. Before doing this, the motifs on the silk are masked by using the same motifs cut out of the paper pattern.

The panel is now finished (see illustration below right). It has been fixed in the pressure-cooker, but we have not soaked it in a bath of turpentine, which would have removed the colouring from the gutta.

You can see that background is no longer flecked. As here it proved not to be satisfactory, it has been replaced by a plain dark brown one which gives more unity to the whole painting.

The panel is then mounted on a piece of plywood.

Drawing the serti with a ruler

Applying colours with a cotton-bud

Finished scarf, page 18

Painting in shades of green

Scarf in colourless gutta

This is a design which has been thought out in advance and drawn free-hand on a pongée of average thickness. A small pipette fitted with a 1-mm diameter nib is used.

Start the design on the left-hand side of the scarf and carry on towards the right. A left-handed person should draw from right to left.

The straight stripes are drawn with a ruler.

The colours are applied using two shades of green and one shade of black.

The shades are blended and lightened with water and alcohol in order to obtain very similar shades but of varying intensity.

The black stripes are made to stand out by decoloration using undiluted alcohol.

The balance of the tones is obtained by darkening certain areas with a mixture of green and black.

The finished scarf is then fixed.

2. Colours which do not run

Brushed paste design

A. Pastes

The characteristic of these pastes is that they do not run through the silk. They enable you to create designs without needing gutta or wax to outline the coloured areas.

With alizarine-based colours it is extremely difficult to obtain large plain areas, at least if they are used undiluted with a brush.

As they are difficult to spread, unbroken lines are hard to achieve. Brush strokes show and must consequently be done with care if you do not want your painting to look a real mess.

To counteract this drawback, several techniques can be used.

● Working with stencils or masks. With this technique, brushes with stiff bristles are used, the paste being applied in dabs. There exist special brushes, called stencil brushes, which look like short-haired shaving brushes.

● Splashing or spraying, which gives a more or less dense flecking. Here again, stencils and masks are used. For this technique, the colour should be diluted in water and should be liquid enough to go through the nozzle of the spray. It can be an aerosol spray, mouth diffuser or airbrush.

Diluted gouaches sprayed on with masks and stencils

● Serigraphy (screen printing). With this technique, the dye is forced through a nylon screen stretched on a frame, using a rubber squeegee. Using serigraphy, you can obtain fine details as well as large plain coloured areas.

These three techniques, like direct painting, require the silk to be mounted on a rigid, absorbent surface.

Mounting the silk

Use a sheet of plywood covered with several layers of absorbent paper such as tissue or kitchen paper.

The silk should be perfectly taut but without losing its shape, which would result in wavy lines after releasing the tension. Attach it to the board using adhesive tape.

We suggest three pieces to illustrate these three techniques.

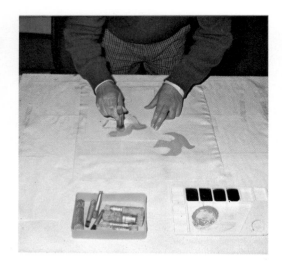

Cushion

Stencils, masks and stencil brushes

The stencil, in the shape of a bird, has been cut out of a sheet of drawing paper using a scalpel.

The blue sky is obtained by blending some turquoise with some white on your palette. The brush is perfectly dry and no water is added.

Start with the light blue, holding the brush in an upright position and dabbing gently.

The colour-gradations are obtained by adding some darker blue at the edges of the motif to get a gradual shading of blues.

Other birds overlap the first ones. They are painted in violet.

Clouds are painted with light blue using a mask with a wavy edge.

Once the painting is finished and dry, the silk is ironed to fix the colours.

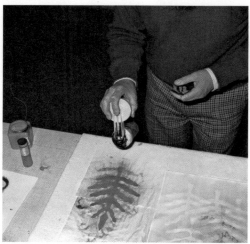

Ferns

Masks and spraying

The mask is cut out of a fairly thick sheet of drawing paper. It represents a stylised fern.

The mask is placed on the silk and the diluted colour is sprayed over it using an aerosol spray. The same process is repeated several times, resulting in a design of white silhouettes in negative against a coloured background.

Then the mask itself is sprayed and immediately applied to the silk, being pressed down firmly. When the mask is removed, its image appears printed in positive on the silk.

Fixing is done by ironing once the colours are dry.

The design is now finished.

You can use natural ferns instead of masks cut out of paper.

Scarf

Serigraphy (screen printing)

The letter A has been chosen as the motif.

Four versions of this letter are drawn with drawing gum on the nylon screen in the frame

Once the drawing gum is dry, a varnish is applied to the whole screen with a squeegee. Any gaps in the varnish are filled with a brush.

Once the varnish is dry, the frame is placed on a flat surface and you can rub off the drawing gum with your fingers. It should come off in little rolls.

You can also use a crêpe rubber.

Once the drawing gum is completely removed, you have a stencil which will reproduce each of the four letters exactly.

After masking three of the four As with adhesive tape, the remaining A is printed by forcing the dye through the screen with a rubber squeegee.

This motif is repeated several times, changing direction and colour.

The same process is used for the other three versions of the letter A.

The border is done with a stencil brush, using the edge of a sheet of paper as a mask.

This example gives a brief insight into the potential of fabric printing using serigraphy. If you are interested in this technique, there are many well-documented books on the subject.

'Old-fashioned' scarf

Stencils, masks, gradated background

We said earlier that it was difficult, not to say impossible, to obtain a plain background with pastes. Yet it *is* possible to do the background in running colours and to complete the design with pastes. This 'old-fashioned' scarf illustrates this technique.

Using the method explained on page 22, the gradated background has been done with a pink paint and the water–alcohol mixture.

The different stencils and masks have been cut out of drawing paper.

Colours are first applied with the stencils using a brush. When the stencil is removed, the design appears clearly without any blotches. Note the shaded tones.

A second stencil is used to paint the curls of smoke. Then the cut-outs of the curls of smoke are themselves used to obtain motifs in negative.

The design is finished. You need only fix it with the iron. Careful! The background should then be fixed by steaming, as the heat of the iron is not strong enough to fix running colours.

Set of masks and stencils

Using a brush to apply colours which do not run with a stencil

Faults and remedies

Certain faults can occur during the application of pastes. Some can be avoided, others corrected.

1. Smudges

When removing the stencil or the screen-printing frame. you may find that colours have smudged and that the drawing is not sharp.

This is caused by an excess of paint or a paint which is too runny.

Prevention: Never work with wet brushes or dilute colours in water. On the contrary, it may be useful to mix them with a thickener or a transparent base to give them more consistency or to reduce their intensity without making them liquid.

Incidentally, it should be noted that it is possible to transform running colours into pastes by mixing them with a special base. They are then like alizarine-based colours. Fixing should still be done by steaming.

Correction: Move the stencil or the frame to shift the edge of the design and thus eliminate the smudge by incorporating it in the motif.

2. Stains

These often occur when placing the stencil or the frame on the fabric.

Indeed, if you are not careful when placing the stencil or the frame on a newly-printed motif, the latter tends to come off on the paper or nylon. Thus, when you remove the stencil or frame. you pick up a stain which will blot the fabric.

In serigraphy, another cause of stains is a poorly-varnished screen. The colour runs through each time it is pushed across the screen with the squeegee to print the motif.

Prevention: Stencil and frame should be placed only on dry or protected motifs.

To protect your motif, use a piece of absorbent paper or the cut-out of the stencil.

In serigraphy, before working on fabric you should first test your screen on a piece of paper to detect any holes and stop them with varnish.

Correction: It is impossible to remove stains. They must be incorporated in your design either by hiding them under a darker colour, or by retouching them to make them part of the design.

Smudges and their correction by moving the stencil

Flower design in gouache

Russian-inspired design in pastels

B. Gouaches and pastels

Gouaches

These are sold in tubes and are diluted in water. Used thick and blended with white, they are applied exactly like gouache on paper.

For gouaches, the fabric should always be stretched on a frame.

Used diluted, they are applied like water-colours. White is not used. Highlights are obtained by playing with the transparency of the colours on the fabric.

Careful! When very dilute, gouaches tend to run through the silk. They should therefore be dabbed on without loading the brush.

This peculiarity is in fact an advantage, as the diluted gouaches can be used with a spray or even with wax to obtain batik effects.

Fixing
Use a hot iron for unstretched fabrics.

Designs on umbrellas should be fixed using a hair-drier on a warm setting.

Designs on lampshades should be fixed automatically by the heat from the bulb.

Protection
All items decorated with gouache which are not washable in soap and water must be coated with an anti-stain varnish which can be bought in spray cans.

Once varnished, they are protected from dust and splashes of water.

This anti-stain varnish can also be used for protecting ties which have been dyed with running colours.

Pastels

Unlike gouaches, pastels should be applied on silk laid on a flat and rigid surface.

With pastels (like wax crayons in shape) it is possible to draw directly on the silk, as is shown by this reproduction of a Russian motif originally carved in wood.

Pastels can give the effect of painting on wood. You should not be afraid of rubbing strongly with the pastel, especially if the design is to be viewed against the light.

Similarly, reliefs can be reproduced simply by placing an uneven surface under the silk and rubbing.

Flowers painted in gouache on wild silk. Note the use of the white in the blue flowers and the highlights of the roses .

Design made by rubbing pastels over autumn leaves through the silk

To obtain a thin, sharp line with pastels, it is necessary to use the transfer technique.

You have only to colour the back of a sheet of paper with pastel and to draw on this piece of paper with a hard pencil or a ball-point pen. The sheet of paper should act as a carbon paper and print onto the fabric.

Fixing
Fixing is done by ironing between two sheets of paper to remove the wax contained in the pastels.

If there are still traces of wax after fixing, remove them as for the removal of gutta, described on page 38.

Transfer drawing with pastel

Flowers

Pastels and gouaches used on the same design

Pastels and gouaches are complementary and can be used together to create a design.

The pastels can even act as a serti and the diluted gouaches can colour the areas between.

The small panel we now describe is a good example.

The pastel is applied to the back of a sheet of paper.

The design is printed on the silk by drawing on this sheet of paper with a pencil. You should obtain a thin, sharp line.

The remaining flowers are drawn directly on the silk with the pastel. The difference in the lines is very clear.

In order to apply the diluted gouache, the silk is stretched on a frame.

The background is done by splashing on some gouache using an oval mask to preserve a blank area for the bunch of flowers.

The drawing is fixed with a hot iron.

Pastels and gouaches are particularly suitable for silk painting by children, as they allow great freedom of expression without too many technicalities.

N.B. Pastels and running colours can also be used together. To prevent them passing through the serti, the serti must be quite thick, and the wax melted with a hair-drier before applying the dyes. The wax is then removed using a hot iron, and the colours fixed by steaming.

C. Felt-tip and ball-point pens

Felt-tip fabric pens

These contain liquid dyestuffs which harden on contact with heat and which run only very slightly, if at all, on silk.

They are for use on silk mounted on a frame, and a whole design can be done in felt pen alone. The colours are exceptionally strong and bright.

They can also be used in conjunction with paints which run. In this hanging they have been used for graphics work over running paints which have been applied direct.

Russian-inspired design created entirely with felt pen on wild silk

Special ball-point pens

As can be seen from the illustration, these are much thicker than ordinary ball-point pens, and have a larger ball at the tip. They contain a thick ink which can be forced down to the ball at the tip by a rubber stopper.

Use them on silk which has been stretched over a smooth, rigid backing, such as a sheet of plywood covered with drawing paper. They can be used only for line drawings.

First, force the ink down by pumping the rubber stopper. Hold the pen upright, pressing lightly to make the ink flow.

Like felt pens, they can be used with paints that run to improve a coloured serti or just to sign a piece of work.

They are fixed with a hot iron.

Ball-point line drawing

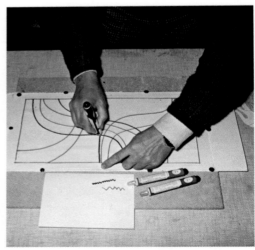

Fixing designs made with paints that run

Running paints are fixed by steaming the decorated silk for a time which varies with the fixing method. Pieces of fabric awaiting fixing must be kept in a dry, dark place.

With a pressure-cooker

This is an ideal method for one-offs. It is useful if, for example, you urgently need a scarf or two or three cushion covers you have decorated. The process is highly effective even though it takes a mere 45 minutes. See pages 43–44.

With a steamer

This method is suited to a large, regular output or where fixing is done for a group of people, such as a fabric design class within a club, for example.

A steamer will not, in fact, pay for itself until after a relatively high number of fixings.

There are two types of steamer on the market: a small-diameter horizontal steamer and the large-capacity vertical one which is described below.

The vertical steamer
This is a double-walled metal cylinder one metre long, into which are inserted the pieces of silk rolled in paper. The cylinder is then placed over a container of boiling water. A domed top with a hole in it caps the cylinder.

The steam rises up the cylinder, penetrating the paper and the fabric on its way, and condenses under the dome. The condensation runs back down between the cylinder's inner and outer walls and into the container to be recycled.

Only a tiny amount of steam escapes through the hole in the dome.

Fixing takes from two to four hours depending on the quantity and type of fabric, although steaming for longer still is far from harmful. A thick fabric requires longer than a thin one.

Rolling the silk in paper
Use a highly porous paper such as lining paper.

The paper is first wrapped a few times around a wooden pole, which will keep the roll rigid, and then stuck with steamproof adhesive tape to stop it unrolling.

The roll of paper is protected by aluminium foil

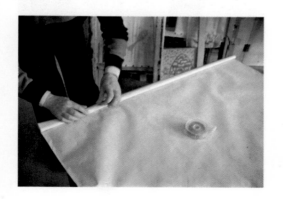

Lay out the pieces of fabric without overlaps or creases to within four centimetres of the edges of the roll.

Take care not to roll up the paper crooked otherwise you could end up with a roll too long to fit in the steamer and have to start all over again.

Once all the pieces of fabric are rolled up, give four more turns before sealing the roll lengthwise with adhesive tape.

The two ends are capped with four layers of aluminium foil taped in place.

This roll is slid vertically into the steamer. It must not on any account be touching the cylinder wall. Use the centring rings to keep the roll properly aligned.

Fit the domed cover.

Place the cylinder over the container of water kept on the boil by a gas burner or an electric ring. Make sure there is plenty of water.

After three hours turn off and allow to cool.

To unroll the fabric, simply reverse the rolling-up procedure. After removing the pieces of silk from the roll, soak them in cold water. The colour may come out slightly, especially with the dark shades, which is why this soaking is done. When the rinsing water is clear, dry the silk and iron.

Technical hitches

These may occur with both the steamer and the pressure-cooker.

A. The paper in which the fabric is wrapped is found to be wet and the silk marked by indelible rings.

Causes
These water stains are due either to poor protection against the dripping condensation or to an insufficient thickness of paper at the end of the roll.

Prevention
1. Check that the foil capping the roll (or covering it in the case of the pressure-cooker) is giving adequate protection and that none of the drips can run off it and onto the paper.
2. Give at least four extra turns of the paper at the end of the roll.
3. With the pressure-cooker, do not overfill or forget the trivet.
4. Do not let the water boil over.

Remedy
There is none. The rings which appear during fixing are indelible.

B. Fabrics decorated with gutta serti stick to the paper, or fabrics decorated with wax still show traces of grease.

Causes
1. the gutta was applied too thickly or was not properly diluted.
2. ironing failed to remove all the wax.

Remedies
In both cases just soak the silk in white spirit. The gutta and wax will dissolve and not a trace of paper or grease will be left on the fabric.

C. The silk has very pronounced creases. This fault usually arises when the pressure-cooker is used for fixing, and is due to the creasing of the roll of paper.

To remove these creases, simply iron the silk once again while it is damp. Several ironings with a steam-iron may be necessary to remove the creases entirely. You can buy a spray-on product which makes this job much easier.

All-purpose paints

We have seen that there are silk dyes with very specific properties and with varying potential for use. The technique had to be adapted to the product and not the opposite or serious disappointments could result. However, a new type of product has recently come onto the market.

These paints have, undiluted, the smooth consistency of non-run paints; when diluted in water they behave like paints which run. They can be toned down without any loss of consistency by using a commercial product. They permit the whole range of special effects: cooking salt or discolouring (with water).

Even serti is made easy because the artificial gutta which completes the range of paints can be applied by pipette or by brush, or even by screenprinting, which is a great advantage.

The paints are fixed with a hot iron.

Moreover, these paints can be used not only on natural fabrics (silk, wool, cotton) but also on synthetic fibres (nylon, tergal, rayon, etc.).

Could this be the solution to all fabric decoration problems? Obviously not, because although they are attractive for their all-purpose use, they cannot compete in depth, brilliance and subtlety of colour with traditional running paints. Also, it is relatively difficult to cover large areas with one colour, although satisfactory results can be obtained by wetting the fabric beforehand.

Despite these facts they are definitely the ideal paints for children. Everything which can be done with alizarine-based paints, gouache and running paints can also be done with these all-purpose paints.

We feel that the 'gutta' is the most interesting product in this new range. We put the term in quotes because it is gutta in name only. The important thing is that it behaves just like gutta.

So we present two examples of what can be done with these products: the first applies 'gutta' with a brush and uses the paints diluted in water, and the second screenprints the 'gutta' and uses traditional running dyes.

Brushing 'gutta' onto fine pongée

The serti is applied straight onto the silk with a brush. Take care not to apply too great a thickness of 'gutta' because on fine silk, which is used here, the lines tend to spread.

Once the 'gutta' is dry, the paints diluted in water are applied in the traditional way, working out from the centre of the areas to be covered.

Brushing gutta onto fine pongée

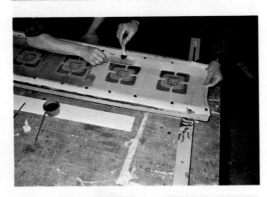

Special effects are achieved with salt on the violet zones.

After drying thoroughly and scraping the salt off carefully with a spoon, iron the silk at the 'silk and wool' setting.

After this ironing, wash the fabric in warm soapy water to remove the 'gutta'. Dry and iron again.

Screenprinting 'gutta' onto moussedoup

Moussedoup has been chosen because it is a fabric whose irregular structure does not lend itself to applying gutta by traditional methods.

The silk is stretched over a layer of absorbent paper.

The screen has been made in the way shown on page 50.

Before the 'gutta' is poured into the screen, check carefully to see that there are no faults in the varnish which seals the nylon which could result in spots of 'gutta' in the wrong places.

Print the serti using a squeegee.

When, as here, a motif is repeated, avoid putting the frame down on the wet 'gutta'. You must either arrange the pattern so that there is no danger of overlap, as has been done here, or wait a while before printing any overlapping motifs.

As soon as the serti has been printed, peel the silk away from the absorbent paper.

Never let the 'gutta' dry on the paper as the paper would be impossible to remove. If this happens the only solution is to soak the silk in water to dissolve the 'gutta' and thereby release the paper. You would then be back to square one, as the 'gutta' would be completely washed away.

The paints are applied in the usual way. Be careful, however, not to go over the 'gutta' line with the paint because in contrast to real gutta, which rejects dyes, the artificial brand absorbs them. The dye has therefore to be applied to the centre of each zone and left to spread to the serti line.

This particular design has a sizeable background with some open areas but also some very narrow parts. For this reason two people have had to work on it together, one doing the delicate parts with a cotton-bud, the other doing the large areas with a pad.

The design is finished and all that remains is to fix it by steaming.

Careful! When the roll is unrolled it is highly likely that the 'gutta' will stay stuck to the paper. Do not try to detach it by pulling away the paper as there is a risk of tearing the silk. Proceed by soaking in water.

Uses for painted silks

Rolled hem, overcast hem and fringes

Scarves

To prevent the silk fraying and to obtain a perfect finish, scarves can be edged with a rolled hem, an overcast hem or a fringe.

But first of all you must remove the part of the silk which has the holes where it was attached to the frame. Do this with scissors, not by tearing the silk.

Cushion covers

1. Only one side of the cushion has been decorated. A matching piece of plain fabric must be found for the back of the cushion.

2. The back and front of the cushion are to be made of a single piece of silk.

In both cases the silk will have to be lined with a white material to bring out the design and give the cover a better appearance.

Sew the silk and the lining on the inside, leaving an opening for the stuffing. Make the corners slightly rounded rather than square.

Turn the pouch which you have made right side out and iron.

Fill the cushion with kapok or pieces of foam rubber. Do not overfill or else the cushion will have no give.

Finally, sew up the opening with a few close stitches.

Decorative panels

There are several ways of mounting decorative silk panels, of which we will illustrate two.

1. Mounting on a rigid backing
For the backing use 9 mm plywood. Make the plywood 6 cm shorter and narrower than the silk to allow for the fact that the silk has to be stapled to the back of the board.

To make the panel stand out and enhance the sheen of the silk, place a layer of polyester wadding between the wood and the silk. The wadding is held in place with double-sided carpet tape.

While the silk is being stapled, it must be kept quite taut – but be careful not to tear it. If despite all precautions a tear starts to appear in a corner of the panel, a drop of clear glue is all that is necessary to make it invisible.

Stapling the silk to the back of the panel after laying the wadding

The painted silk backed with adhesive Bristol board is mounted on the frame

2. Mounting for a wall-hanging

There are two possibilities:

a) The silk panel is unlined

What are to be the vertical sides of the panel must be rolled or hemmed.

What are to be the horizontal sides are glued between two pieces of half-round dowelling or gripped in the jaws of a strip of plastic binding.

b) The silk panel is lined

Pieces of round dowel are inserted into the gap left between the silk and the lining in the top and bottom hems.

In both cases the dowel must extend at least 5 cm beyond the silk on either side. The panel is hung with a cord attached to the ends of the top dowel.

Lampshades

Decorated silk is well suited to the making of lampshades. The best results are obtained by using a thin card or plastic backing for the silk and metal hoops without uprights.

The 'hoops' may be, as their name suggests, circular as well as oval, square or oblong.

The size of the backing must be measured exactly. Its length will be equal to the circumference of the circle plus 1 cm for gluing. Its width will correspond to the height of the finished shade.

You must beware of getting bubbles or creases in the silk when sticking it down. The silk should extend 1 cm beyond the adhesive at top and bottom.

This strip is turned in and stuck down to hide the metal frame. Use a transparent, water-free glue to stick the backing to the frame.

Edging ribbon adds the finishing touch.

Clothing

Dresses, tunics, blouses and ties can all be made out of painted silk.

To go into detail about these creations would be to go beyond the scope of this book. But you must remember that the different parts of the article must be drawn, decorated and fixed before any cutting is done at all.